Brave for my Family

By Davidson Whetstone

Illustrated by his father

Foreward by
David R. Shedd

"The true soldier fights not because
he hates what is in front of him, but because he
loves what is behind him."

– G.K. Chesterton

---·····---

Davidson's story of deep love for God, family and country is profound yet simply told from the heart of a seven year old.

The sacrifice of those left behind at home – the families – while the warfighter deploys to the front lines in defense of our freedoms is brought to life in this narrative.

Uncertainty of the unknown but undergirded by a deep faith for sustainment should swell our hearts with gratitude for every boy and girl whose daddy or mommy is responding to a call to service greater than self.

Davidson reminds us with such clarity why we should ask God to bless America.

May He watch over every warfighter _and_ family member who rises up every day recognizing that sacrifice is necessary so that we might enjoy the liberties that we hold dear.

Thank you Davidson for sharing your heart.

David R. Shedd,
Former Acting Director of the Defense Intelligence Agency

Hello, my name is Davidson. I like Legos.
My Dad is in the Army, he is a Green
Beret.

A Green Beret trains in America by shooting guns, jumping out of airplanes, and learning to speak different languages.

They are tough, strong, and brave.

Dad went to Afghanistan. I felt sad.

He had to go to Afghanistan because it was his turn to fight terrorists.

Mommy was sad too.

I hugged my Dad goodbye.

Then we prayed.

I did not know if he was going to come back. I prayed every night that he would come back.

Even though I was still sad, I had fun because I got to visit Grandaddy and Grandmama in Boston. My Grandaddy got me a donut. It was a chocolate donut with green and brown sprinkles, just like the Army. I rode my bike too. It was a Mickey Mouse bike. I liked to eat my donut with Grandaddy when he read the Bible and drank his coffee.

My Grandpa pulled me in the sleigh when I was in Vermont for Thanksgiving. My Grandpa and I saw a Black Bear. The next day I made gingerbread cookies with Gogo, my Grandma.

Isaiah 40:3

DJS 2004

Four days before Christmas, after gymnastics, my Mom got a phone call that my Dad got wounded when he was fighting terrorists. My Mom cried and I was pretty scared that my Dad was going to die. We got on an airplane to Washington, DC.

While my Dad was in surgery we found an apartment. We put our things there. Then we went to Walter Reed and I saw my Dad. I hugged him because I was so happy that he was alive.

We had a special guest. It was Vice President Biden. We travelled to Washington D.C. and saw the museums. I even saw the White House.

My Dad brought me to the Washington,

D.C. Vietnam Memorial Wall.

I saw all the names on the wall.

Gave proof through the night that ou
O! say does that star, spangle ba
O'er the land of the free &
the home of the brave?

My dad and I went to the flag that flew over Fort McHenry, and my Mom was there too, and my brother.

We also went to the Arlington National Cemetery. We walked and saw the Tomb of the Unknown Soldier. It is guarded by the Old Guard; they guard it through the night and day, even in storms.

It is good to be respectful.

Pentagon City

I had so much fun with my family in Washington, D.C. Then we went to the Metro. It said "Doors closing, step back!" – the door was actually closing!

When I looked out of the window, everything looked like lines.

We went to the zoo. I saw a rhino and a tiger. I saw a lion. It was so fierce! There was blood on his teeth and on his claws. He stood on a rock, and his teeth were so sharp.

I went to Medieval Times. I saw a Crusader – it's a knight. It looked like the good knight was losing, but he was not. Right at the last second, he jumped up and grabbed his sword and defeated the bad knight.

While my Dad was in the hospital, the terrorists killed his friend in Afghanistan, so he had to go back to fight them. I felt so sad and angry. I did not know if he would get wounded again. When my Dad got better, the doctor said he could go back to Afghanistan.

He left on an airplane from Boston to Ft. Bragg. Then he got on a C-17 to go back to the war. I hugged my Dad and he hugged me. I miss my Dad when he leaves. I pray for him everyday. I know that he prays for me too. I can't wait until he comes back home.

While he is gone

I stay brave for my family.

We had a specia
guest it was Vice
President.
Biden.
We traveled to
Washington DC
and saw the
museums.
I even saw the wi
house. My Dad brot
me to the Washingt
DC Vietnam memorial
Wall I saw all the names
on the Wall. Me and my Dad
went to the Flag that flew
over fort McHenry and my m
were there too and brother. We olso went to
the Arlengton nashonln cemetery.

How did family help Davidson get through his father's deployment?

Davidson prayed every night knowing that his dad was saying the same prayers and praying for him. He also watched videos that his dad made for him reading some of Davidson's favorite books. His dad would send pictures of him and some of Davidson's friends (stuffed animals) all over Afghanistan.

How does everyone in a military family serve our country?

Some of the greatest sacrifices that soldiers make are ones that most people outside the military don't always think of. Davidson's dad missed his first words, his first steps, first Christmas, and his first birthday on Davidson's first deployment. His dad just completed his 9th deployment. His mom has traveled across the country and moved the whole family by herself. The best parts of being in a family are what military families sacrifice, but without his family, Davidson's dad could never serve the way he does. Davidson's whole family serves our country.

What can you do for a kid whose parents are serving in the military?

Be friends to kids whose parents are in the military. Military kids have to move a lot, so they are always the new kids at school and church. Their birthday parties have different friends each year, and they don't always get invited to other people's parties because they are new. They have to say goodbye to best friends a lot. Being friendly to kids with parents in the military means a lot.

If you can do anything that gives that family a special time together, that is nice. One time, a friend of Davidson's dad let their family stay at a really nice place where the family had a vacation.

What characters of bravery did Davidson encounter during his father's recovery?

Davidson met a little girl at the Walter Reed Hospital playground whose father had lost his legs, fingers, and eyesight in an IED explosion. Her dad brought her to the playground with her grandparents to play. Even though he couldn't run around the playground with her, he was brave for being there for her even when it was hard for him.

Davidson Whetstone has moved 9 times in his young life and attended 3 different schools. He finished writing this book in 1st grade and started 3rd grade in 2019. He likes drawing, writing, history, soccer, wrestling, legos and Bible study. Like his father, Davidson writes and draws to think through tough memories in his life. Sometimes it is hard to talk about some things, but it is easier to write about them. Davidson hopes this story will help other kids know that there are a lot of military kids who serve our country, and they are not alone.

PROCEEDS OF THIS BOOK support Military Families and Wounded Warriors through trusted organizations who have demonstrated their commitment to serving those who serve. We would like to thank the Green Beret Foundation, Rick Herrema Foundation, Lead The Way Fund, Navy SEAL Foundation, Semper Fi Fund and the Patriot Foundation for the valuable work they do.

www.greenberetfoundation.org

Rick Herrema Foundation
www.rhfnow.org

www.leadthewayfund.org

www.navysealfoundation.org

www.semperfifund.org

www.patriotfoundation.com